# Creative
# Containers
## for
# Geocaching

## Vince Migliore

Blossom Hill Books

i

Title: 3904768


Title:   **Creative Containers for Geocaching**

Description: **Creative Containers for Geocaching** is a how-to guide for creating cache containers used in geocaching.

ISBN-13:  978-1477635711

ISBN-10:  1477635718

Primary Category: Sports & Recreation / General
Country of Publication: United States
Language: English
Search Keywords: geocaching, crafts, containers, treasure hunting
Author: Vince Migliore

Blossom Hill Books
113 Sombrero Way
Folsom, California 95630 USA

Reorder:  https://www.createspace.com/**3904768**

First Edition, June 2012

Blossom Hill Books, 113 Sombrero Way, Folsom, CA 95630

# Table of Contents

Introduction ............................................................... 1

1. The Bison Tube ...................................................... 7
2. Film Canister ......................................................... 13
3. Food Jar ................................................................. 17
4. Food Storage Container ..................................... 23
5. Military Ammunition Can .................................. 27
6. Water Bottles and Thermos Containers ........... 33
7. Toys as Cache Containers ................................... 37
8. PVC Tubing Cache ............................................... 41
9. False Sprinkler ..................................................... 47
10. Key Holder .......................................................... 51
11. Hollowed Out Log .............................................. 55
12. Birdhouse Conversion ...................................... 61
13. False Surveillance Camera ............................... 67
14. Library Book ........................................................ 71
15. False Utility Box .................................................. 81
16. Magnetically Sealed Enclosure ........................ 87
17. Concrete Mold ..................................................... 93
18. Sheet Metal Cache Wrap ................................... 99
19. Hand Crank Electric Light ................................ 105

Appendices ............................................................. 119

# Introduction

This book is designed to present projects and ideas for making outstanding containers and hides for geocaching. If you love geocaching as much as I do, then sooner or later you will want to make a contribution to the hobby by creating an enjoyable experience for others.

John Lennon, the philosophical songwriter for The Beatles, once wrote "In the end, the love you take is equal to the love you make." The same is true for our hobby: you get out of it just about what you put into it. In geocaching, one of the most enjoyable adventures is to find a cache that brings a smile to the searcher's face, or perhaps a raised eyebrow for the craftsmanship that went into its construction. If you want to just get by with minimal effort, then wash out an old mayonnaise jar, but if you want to elevate the sport and spread the cheer of creating a memorable cache, then take the little effort required to make a truly creative cache container.

**Fun for the searcher**

Many factors contribute to making a memorable cache. It might be that the name of the street and the type of container match each other, such as an apple-shaped jar hidden on McIntosh Street. It might be that the route to the location takes you past an awesome vista. Or it might be that the mental gymnastics needed to solve a field puzzle gives an extra punch to the cache. All such considerations help make the experience enjoyable, but one of the biggest fun factors is making an eye-caching or clever container.

Containers can be fun, frivolous, crafty, or mechanical. They should enhance the geocaching experience by adding variety and artistry to the hiding place. Even a simple upgrade makes a big difference, **Figure 1**.

**Design Considerations**

Many practical matters can limit our creativity, such as the expense, the availability of materials, time considerations, and the crafting skills of the cache owner.

In addition to creative ideals, we have to think about the following design concerns:

1. Waterproofing. Water contamination is probably the most common problem facing cache owners. Even with sealable containers, water often works its way in and makes for a soggy log. Waterproof papers are now available, but they are expensive. A good solution to the water problem is to add layers of protection. You might, for example, have a bird house as the outer layer and camouflage exterior, then have a Tupperware container inside the bird house, and then again have the log sealed inside a plastic bag.

2. Stealth. You want your cache to be searchable and recognizable by the geocacher, but mundane enough to pass as an ordinary part of the environment for non-cachers (muggles).

3. Accessibility. The cache may endure quite a bit of traffic, so the container must open and close easily, have a decent seal, and be hidden in such a way it can easily be returned to its hiding place.

4. Sturdiness. The cache must hold contents securely, be able to withstand weather and mechanical buffeting, and survive long enough to minimize changing of the container.

5. Ease of Production. Creativity is great, but not always practical. I found a hollow log in a pet store that costs only $12.00. It was made for the bubble-maker for fish tanks. It might take 3 or 4 hours to hollow out the same sized log with drills and chisels, but the store bought version works just as well in hiding the container.

With these considerations in mind, the next step is to honestly assess your level of skill and patience with mechanical processes, such as drilling holes, soldering, or painting. Although it's good once in a while to stretch yourself, it's also wise to know your limits. If you don't know how to change the blades on a Dremmel tool (or even know what a Dremmel tool is), then you might want to stick with buying a simple Tupperware container and using your artistic skills to paint a design on the outside. On the other hand, if you have a 3-car garage converted to a world class wood shop, then you can go ahead and tackle something more creative.

Figure 1. Containers don't have to be complicated to be interesting. Here a jar inside a tin or a vegetable holder with eyes glued onto it does the trick.

# 1.   The Bison Tube

A bison tube is a small metal cylinder with a screw-off top and waterproof seal. It can range in size from about 3/8-inch wide and 2-3/8-inch long to 1-inch wide and 3-inches long. The most common size is a half inch wide and 2-3/4-inch long. Thus, it can usually hold nothing but a rolled up log sheet. The tubes come with a keychain type slip ring, so they are easily attached to other objects.

| Name | **The Bison Tube** |
|------|--------------------|
| Description | Small screw-top metallic container |
| Pros | Inexpensive, works well, small size |
| Cons | Waterproofing is only fair |
| Appeal | Low appeal, but easily spiced up |
| Cost | Minimal; about $1.00 each |
| Time | Under 15 minutes |
| Difficulty | Easy |

Project summary: Bison tubes.

Bison tubes generally cost about a dollar each, with large discounts for bulk purchases. They have a very small rubber seal that can wear out in a short time. This can compromise its waterproofing ability. These tubes are best used where a second layer of protection can be added against the rain. For example, you can put them inside a steel fence post cap or inside a piece of PVC pipe.

**Figure 2** shows some ways to make the hide more interesting. At top, a metal fence post cap has been drilled to take a #6 machine screw and nut, which is glued on the inside and attached by a plastic tie. You don't really need to drill a hole it the top, as the glue generally holds well, but a mechanical connection is always better than glue alone.

In the center is a hack-sawed railroad tie with a bison tube attached to the end. Old, rusty railroad ties can be found on line, or if you're lucky and live in a town with an abandoned rail line you can find them at nearby flea markets. Obviously, do not hide or retrieve anything on an active rail line.

To make a railroad spike cache, prop the railroad tie into a vise and cut it in half with a hacksaw. Next saw a groove in the cut end. Insert a wire in the groove then put masking tape around the end. This holds the wire in place and forms a cup for the glue. Pour in epoxy or gorilla glue to provide an anchor for the wire that holds the bison tube.

At the bottom, a bison tube is placed inside a toy rubber duck. It doesn't take much effort to find toys and fun items to act as outer camouflage for the bison tubes.

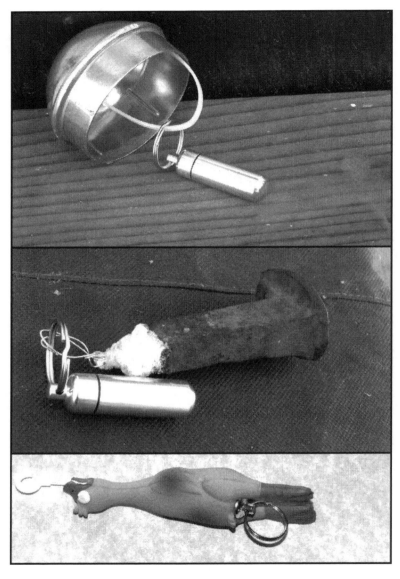

Figure 2. These are examples of bison tube hides.

Bison tubes are pretty versatile, as they fit inside many outdoor objects, such as pipes, fences, knotholes in trees, and as a hanger on bushes. A bison tube is easily made into a hanger by wrapping a bread tie or a paper clip through the slip ring and hanging it on the inner limb of a tree or shrubbery.

A variation on the bison tube is the "nano" tube. These are generally much smaller, about a half-inch long and a quarter-inch wide. They contain tiny rolled up log sheets which often require a tweezers to remove from the cylinder. They are usually magnetic and will stick to the back of a traffic sign, under a bench, or attached to any metallic surface.

Nano tubes get mixed reviews from geocachers. On the one hand, being so small they are easy to hide in urban settings and can be a challenge to find. On the other hand, they don't allow trading of travel bugs and the logs fill up quickly.

# 2. Film Canister

A film canister refers to the plastic 35-mm film containers most photographers are familiar with. The black film containers are constructed of high density polyethylene (HDPE) plastic, a tough, commonly used semi-rigid material. Its flexibility allows the cap to be pushed on and removed by hand for a decent seal against moisture. Like the bison tubes, it's best to provide an extra layer of protection against moisture. This category includes other common containers of similar size. **Figure 3** shows a slightly smaller medical supply container with a flip-top cap. This is recycled from the can for diabetic test strips.

| Name | **Film Canister** |
|------|-------------------|
| Description | Small plastic pop-top containers |
| Pros | Inexpensive, works well, small size |
| Cons | Seal wears out after a while |
| Appeal | Low appeal, but easily enhanced |
| Cost | Minimal; about $1.00 each |
| Time | Under 15 minutes |
| Difficulty | Easy |

Project summary: Film canisters.

Containers for 35-mm film are 1-7/8-inch long and 7/8 inch in diameter. These containers are quite common in geocahing. You can simply add a bent paper clip and some camouflage tape and have an instant hanging hide. Hopefully we can take it one step further and make something interesting out of it.

One of the easiest things you can do is paint a face on the cap, or the entire body, to make it look like a bug or animal. If the lid is the face of a cat, for example, you can glue on eyes and whiskers. I find epoxy glue works best for this type of add-on.

You can also insert the film canister into a toy, into a camouflaging object, or simply attach it to the back of a model truck as in the photo.

Figure 3. There are several methods of spicing up a simple film canister cache.

# 3. Food Jar

Jars are probably the most popular form of container for geocaching. Cleaned up mayonnaise and peanut butter jars are most common, as they come in large sizes and have a lid, or mouth, that is as wide as the jar itself. They provide good water-proofing and the only cost you endure is washing out the last vestiges of food content.

| Name | Food Jar |
| --- | --- |
| Description | Used food and liquid containers |
| Pros | Cheap, everywhere, wide mouth |
| Cons | A bit on the boring side |
| Appeal | Available everywhere; need to add appeal |
| Cost | Next to nothing |
| Time | Quick and easy |
| Difficulty | Easy; You need to add craft ideas |

Project summary: Augmenting the appearance of food jars.

A crucial variable with jars is that they must have a good seal to keep out water. Many good jars have spongy plastic or rubber cushioning that seals against water as you tighten the lid. Some plastic jars can be quite thin and corrode over time. It's best to pick a jar with a good seal and think walls.

## Plastic versus glass jars

I know glass is frowned upon because of the danger of breakage, but some jars are quite thick and strong, and many environments, such as deserts and deep forest have few rock hazards that pose a danger of breakage. The rule of thumb is to use plastic instead of glass. Just imagine your search area covered with chards of broken glass and you get the idea.

Glass can be stronger and more durable and you might choose that route IF:

- The glass is tempered and tough, like Pyrex®.
- The entire container is covered with a layer or two of protective tape.
- The glass container is completely surrounded by a protective outer layer, such as a glass jar inside a wooden birdhouse.

In a nutshell, the glass jar must be protected in such a way that even if it breaks the chards will not pose a danger. You can assist in this goal by embedding it in an outer protective shell, such as a wooden frame.

*Pyrex* is a registered trademark of Corning, Inc., Corning, NY.

Figure 4. Plastic containers and jars come in all sizes.

**Figure 4** shows some examples of jars. At top is a pop-up lid container, a metal screw cap on a glass jar, and medicine bottle-sized plastic screw top container.

The middle illustration shows the inner lining which provides the seal against water. The bottom illustrates the difficulty with jars – that is, they are hard to dress up and make interesting. Sometimes the best you can do is simply to cover them with a toy or outer mask. The bottom portion of the photo shows jars covered with patterned duct tape.

Here are some ideas for making the containers more interesting:

- Paint a scene on the inside of the plastic container, then seal the design with urethane spray to protect it.
- Cover the jar with duct tape or camouflage tape. Duct tape now comes in several different colors and designer patterns, such as leopards' skin and zebra stripes.
- Use craft wire to add legs, arms, antennas and such to the outside, and secure it with a good quality glue, such as epoxy.

Have fun. Jars represent a quick and easy way to get started with your first cache hide.

# 4. Food Storage Container

Food storage containers are popular cache holders. We are referring to plastic sealable containers such as Tupperware® and Rubbermaid®. One of the most popular types of food containers for caches is known as Lock & Lock which has sealing latches on all four sides of the lid.

| Name | **Food Storage Container** |
| --- | --- |
| Description | Durable, sealable food storage containers |
| Pros | Made to be tough and waterproof |
| Cons | Seal wears out in outdoor environments |
| Appeal | Convenient but not very appealing |
| Cost | $2 to $5 each |
| Time | Quick and easy |
| Difficulty | Easy to work with but needs spicing up |

Project summary: Tupperware, Rubbermaid Food Storage.

The chief advantages of this type of cache are their excellent seal against moisture, and the variety of sizes they come in. Another advantage is that they are easily covered with paint or camouflage material.

*Rubbermaid* is a registered trademark of Rubbermaid Commercial Products, Inc, Wooster, OH. *Tupperware* is a registered trademark of DART Industries, Inc., Orlando, FL.

## Variations

The four-edged Lock & Lock type containers are produced by other manufacturers as shown in **Figure 5**. In the center photo, a Pyrex® cup is shown with a sealable rubber lid. The bottom portion shows 4-latch sealed containers in the field, the left one painted a camouflage color and the right left unaltered.

Figure 5. Food storage containers make good caches.

# 5. Military Ammunition Can

The ammo can, or ammunition container, is a classic and popular cache hide. It has a relatively large storage capacity and it's rugged and waterproof.

| Name | **Military Ammunition Can** |
|---|---|
| Description | Ammunition Container |
| Pros | Tough, spacious, waterproof |
| Cons | Old seals can leak, hard to hide |
| Appeal | Popular but cumbersome |
| Cost | $10 to $30 |
| Time | Little time required |
| Difficulty | Easy to moderate depending on add-ons. |

Project summary: Military ammo can.

There are several variations on the ammo can. Some are original World War II surplus containers. These generally have poor water seals that have dried out over the years. Fortunately they are easy to repair with thin weather stripping. Although they provide a fairly good seal, water often does find a way to get into the box. Some are modern plastic versions which are not as strong as the metal type. Others are odd sizes for different calibers of ammunition.

The standard size is the classic .50 caliber M2A1 which is 7 1/4" high, 5 3/4" wide, and 11" long, **Figure 6**. They weigh about 5 pound each or a little more for shipping purposes. The other standard sizes you might see are .30 caliber, 25mm, 40mm, or the "tall" version which is 6" by 11" by 13".

**Hiding the Ammo Can**

The ammo can, being fairly large, is a favorite for geocachers who want to trade items or to make a cache that will serve as a travel-bug hotel. The upside of large containers is that they can hold much more interesting trade and swag items, but the downside is that they are more easily discovered by passers-by, or "muggles" who might compromise the hide.

**Swag** is a short-hand word for the toys and tradable items found it caches. It comes from S.W.A.G, meaning stuff we all get, referring to the gifts that celebrities receive at red-carpet events. **Muggles**, the term used in Harry Potter movies for non-wizards, refers to people who are not aware that the enclosure is part of the geocaching game.

Since the ammo box is so large, it's important to hide it among rocks or vegetation that can help conceal its square outline. A good way to both hide it and make it simple is to use a mask type cover, such as the wraps described elsewhere, **Chapter 18**. In **Figure 6** I used sheet metal flowers to hide the cache. You'd be surprised how effective something that simple is when used in the field.

Figure 6. Top: Ammo boxes have a lever-like latch.
Bottom: Simple metal foil wrap works well in the woods.

A more thorough way to hide the box is to surround it with rocks or cover the top with moss or other artificial flower type decorations.

# 6. Water Bottles and Thermos Containers

Sports-type water bottles, seal-top coffee mugs and thermos containers are everywhere. They make great cache hide because they seal well, are relatively rugged, and are inexpensive.

| Name | Water Bottles and Thermos Containers |
| --- | --- |
| Description | Water bottles and drink containers |
| Pros | Easy and cheap |
| Cons | Hard to dress up |
| Appeal | Appeal depends on what you do with it |
| Cost | $2 to $15 |
| Time | Quick and easy |
| Difficulty | Relatively easy |

Project summary: Screw-top water bottles and thermos containers.

Sports drink containers, water bottles, thermos cups and the like are everywhere and are easily converted to a waterproof cache. The only difficulty is that most of them have a flip up spout or opening for a straw that has to be sealed up. That leaves just the screw-off top to provide access to the cache. For me the glue of choice is epoxy.

Many of these containers have hooks (for a bicycle) or clips that can be used as hangers for the cache. They come in a variety of colors, so black or green will help with concealment. As with jars and other off-the-shelf containers the trick here is to add something to the outside to make it more appealing, more camouflaged, or more theme-specific for the searcher.


## Simple Camouflage

**Figure 7** shows two unadorned drink containers at the top; the left one made of metal and the right a simple flip-top plastic container. You will notice the plastic container also has a screw-off lid. Both have hooks convenient for hanging.

At the bottom left is a small thermos completely covered in camouflage tape, and at the bottom right a two-layer coffee mug with a ghost figurine attached to the top. The same glue that secures the figurine to the top also seals the flip-up spout shut.

Figure 7. Sport drink containers and thermos bottles make great caches.

There are two basic approaches to make the plain containers more interesting. First, you can add colored tape to the outside, paint the outside with designs, such as teeth or a face, or add texture with thick paint and additions, such as glitter or sand. The second approach is to add objects to the outside that transform the shape or appearance. For example you can add wire legs to make it look like a bug, or wings to make it look like a bird or plane. If the container is going to hang in a bush or a tree, simply adding artificial leaves or bark to the outside will completely transform its appearance.

The trouble with adding things like legs to the outside is the difficulty of attaching objects to hard, durable surfaces such as metal or plastic. I find it best to add secure anchors, such as copper wire or plastic zip ties to the outside then apply a waterproof glue to keep them in place. You can then attach decorations to the wire or zip ties.

# 7. Toy Cache Containers

Toys make great cache containers because the shape and purpose of the toy easily lends itself to an amusing hiding place. You can use a child's action figure to hold a container and that's enough to make it interesting. You can use the space inside toys to hide more traditional containers.

| Name | **Toys as Cache Containers** |
|---|---|
| Description | Any toy with a hollow inside is a cache |
| Pros | Very easy and quick to engineer |
| Cons | Not the best camouflage |
| Appeal | Fun, especially for children |
| Cost | Minimal; usually under $5.00 |
| Time | Very fast; under 30 minutes |
| Difficulty | Quite simple |

Project summary: Toys as hiding containers.

## A Quick and Simple Transformation

Sturdy plastic or rubber toys are good for hides. I particularly like dog toys and pool toys because they are generally rugged and nearly waterproof.

The very simplest arrangement is to attach a toy to a container, making it appear the toy is carrying or riding the container. In the photo below **Figure 8**, a toy cricket is holding a screw-top jar, and a tree face toy mold shows you can transform any container into a cartoon-like head. These tree faces are found in garden stores. Similar faces are made for pumpkins at Halloween.

In the lower part of the photograph a rubber dog toy in the shape of a tree is easily modified to hold a plastic jar. The bottom portion of the dog's throw toy is cut open to remove the squeaker, and a hole is punched in the top to add a hanger wire. The toy is in the shape of a tree limb, so this would work well for hides within the branches of a tree.

This type of cache is super-simple and quick to make. The rubber is stiff and durable enough that even with the split in the bottom the toy retains its shape and closes over onto the container.

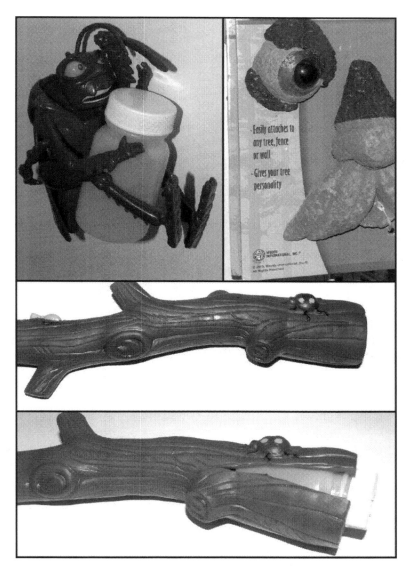

Figure 8. You can make quick and easy conversions of toys for cache hides.

# 8.  PVC Tubing Cache

If you haven't worked with PVC tubing before, you're in for a treat. PVC, short for polyvinyl chloride, is a light-weight material that lends itself well to cache hides because it is cheap, easy to cut, and it comes in a variety of sizes. In addition, the ends of the tube can be covered with a slip-on cap or a threaded lid that provides a water tight seal.

| Name | **PVC Tubing Cache** |
|------|------------------------|
| Description | Standard PVC pipe used for a container |
| Pros | Cheap, easy to work with, blends well |
| Cons | White PVC damaged by the sun |
| Appeal | It often looks like a utility pipe |
| Cost | Very affordable |
| Time | Quick and easy |
| Difficulty | Good beginner project |

Project summary: PVC piping cache.

Most people are familiar with the ½-inch and ¾-inch tubing used for home sprinkler systems. These of course are adequate for hiding small bison tubes or nano containers. There are, however, much larger sizes, such as 3-inch to over 12-inch diameter pipes. When you combine that with the pre-fitted end caps and the ability to cut the pipe to any length, you can see this is a good solution for custom cache sizes.

You can also easily paint PVC, drill holes for handles and attachments, and use adapters to transition from one size to another. Another advantage is that PVC piping is so common that when you position it next to a utility box or construction site, it seems to fit right in, looking like a part of the facility engineering.

## The basic container

I find that the standard black 3-inch black (sewer pipe) is a great way to start. The black color blends in easily, and the 3-inch size is still pretty inexpensive. Spend some time in the hardware store looking at all the attachments and gismos that go with the basic design. The minimum you'll need is a section of tubing, a slip-on cap for one end, and a screw-on cap for the other end. You will need to buy a small tube of PVC glue, as well, to seal the slip-on cap in place. Since the basic pipe does not come with a threaded end, you will have to buy a slip-on cap with a threaded interior, and a threaded plug to allow geocachers to open the container. You can use an unglued slip on cap for the open end too, but it will not be as watertight as the screw cap.

If you want to seal one end permanently, use a small can of PVC glue. Select a medium grade, such as the green can.

Figure 9. PVC piping and connectors come in various sizes.

**Figure 9** shows some of the many shapes for the ¾-inch PVC pipes, with an elbow, an end cap, and an extension connector that has one slip-on side and one side that's threaded to take a threaded plug. The great advantage of PVC caches is that you can choose large size tubes, as show in the lower portion of the photograph. Here the familiar sewer pipe access cap is pictured, the classic black version as well as a white alternative. You might want to consider buying a flange connector too for the bottom of the tube. It allows you to mount the pipe on any piece of wood, so that when you deposit the cache in the wild, it looks as if it's a utility pipe coming out of the ground.

# 9. False Sprinkler

False sprinkler heads are a fairly common hiding place for caches, but they remain quite popular. Essentially, you take out the insides of the sprinkler head, seal the top and bottom ends, and you have a simple screw-off top container for hiding items. The sprinklers come in all different sizes, so you can choose a larger one if you want to fit more inside.

| Name | **False Sprinkler Head** |
|------|--------------------------|
| Description | Garden sprinklers with insides removed |
| Pros | Easily altered, great natural camouflage |
| Cons | Not very waterproof |
| Appeal | Good for instant camouflage |
| Cost | Inexpensive; under $10 |
| Time | Under 15 minutes |
| Difficulty | Easy |

Project summary: False sprinklers.

There are some warnings you should remember if you choose this method. First, don't damage private property or public lands. This means you will have to either be the owner or get written permission from the owner to dig the hole where the sprinkler will be placed. Second, the sprinkler head has two openings, one at the top and one at the bottom, and both need to be sealed. Finally, if there is a garden or shrubbery around, you want to warn seekers not to trample plants or vegetation in their search.

If you're not familiar with sprinklers, get an old or broken one to play with. They are designed to let water in from the bottom, connected to underground PVC piping, and spray it out the top. Sprinkler heads come in all different lengths and diameters. Remember, you will have to dig a hole to place the device, so consider that when choosing a size.

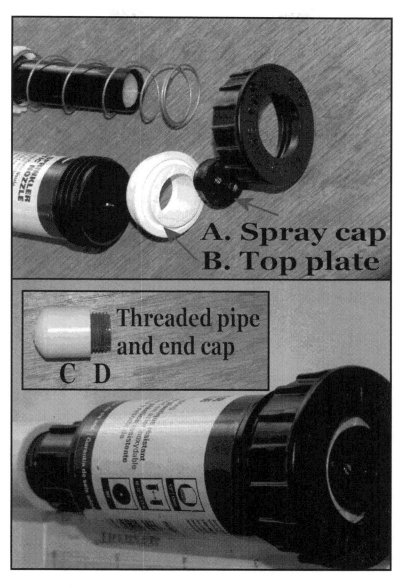

A. Spray cap
B. Top plate

Threaded pipe and end cap
C  D

Figure 10. This is a false sprinkler head. Discard the riser and the spring, but save the cap and the cover pieces (top). Seal the bottom end with threaded tubing and cap.

There is a spring-loaded riser inside, and as you unscrew the top, the spring will push the riser channel out. And yes, you can knock your eye out.

Unscrew the top and remove the riser and spring. The riser tube has a simple screw-off spray cap. Remove that from the riser tube. Discard the riser tube and the spring that surrounds it. There may also be a top plate in the removable cap. See **Figure 10,** items A and B. Replace the cap into the top plate and pour a small amount of epoxy glue into it to seal the holes. Set that aside and let the glue dry.

You will have to buy a small section of threaded PVC tubing and a threaded cap for the bottom end to seal it. See **Figure 10**, items C and D. Hand tighten the bottom to seal that end. When the glue is dry on the top part, simply screw on the lid again and you're good to go. You will have to dig a small hole in the ground to place it. You want just the top of the sprinkler to be visible.

Now, if you're incredibly lazy – and I shouldn't even mention this – there are ready-make key hiders in the shape of a phony sprinkler head available in many hardware stores. These are truly ready to go and the ends are sealed already, but they don't look as authentic as the re-engineered ones we've just described.

# 10. Key Holder

Key holders or hiders refer to those containers you can buy at most hardware stores that are designed to hide a spare set of keys for your house. They are usually in the shape of a rock, yard animal, or a simple metal box that has magnets on the back. This category includes other common off-the-shelf products, such as hollow rocks, light weight boulders for hiding a garden hose, or flower pots in the shape of stones and animals.

| Name | **Key Holders** |
|------|-----------------|
| Description | Objects designed to hide house keys |
| Pros | Ready to go off the shelf |
| Cons | Not very waterproof |
| Appeal | Good for instant camouflage |
| Cost | Moderate; can range from $2 to $25 |
| Time | Under 15 minutes |
| Difficulty | Easy |

Project summary: Key holders.

This type of cache is the lazy man's solution to hiding a cache, and you generally don't have to do much to improve its appearance. The key-hide containers are usually not waterproof, so you will need to add another inside container or at least a sealable plastic bag for the log book.

There are some easy fixes for the magnetic key holder. One simple improvement is to blot out the manufacturer's logo with black paint and add white stick-on numbers to the front. Cover this with a couple layers of spray-on urethane for moisture protection. The letters allow you to stick the box right onto any metallic surface and it looks like a registration or identification number. See **Figure 11** top.

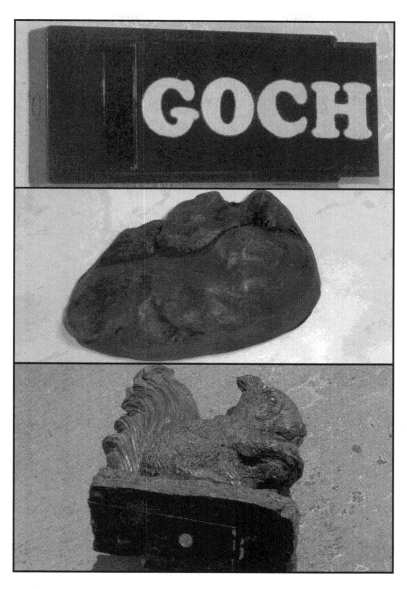

Figure 11. Disguised key holders come in many shapes, including the standard magnetic key holder, dog-doo hide, and garden animal.

The hollow rock and dog-doo key holders probably don't need any adjustments. If they are hidden among rocks or debris of the same color they will blend in nicely. See **Figure 11** center. If you want to add a personal touch, look for "textured" spray paints. These are extra thick spray cans, about $6.00 each, that leave a textured finish. The same holds true for the larger false boulders designed to cover hoses or utility meters. These are generally recognized as props once you are close up, but in a field of similar rock or landscape materials, they can be great places to hide caches.

There are also quite a number of garden animal key holders, such as turtles, squirrels, and gnomes that double as key holders. See **Figure 11** bottom. Again, these don't need much work, but they are generally small and can hold only a log and the smallest swag items, such as coins.

# 11. Hollowed Out Log

The idea here is to hide a cache in the woods using a wooden log that mimics a broken or cut limb of a tree. The cache then is placed with other logs, branches and debris so that it blends in with the environment.

This can be a difficult project because wood is tough, heavy, and it can splinter and crack.

| Name | Hollowed Out Wooden Log |
|---|---|
| Description | Broken or sawed off tree limb |
| Pros | Blends in nicely in a forest setting |
| Cons | Requires muscle, tools, and perspiration |
| Appeal | Very natural in appearance, good hide |
| Cost | Inexpensive; may need to buy tools |
| Time | 2 to 4 hours |
| Difficulty | Moderate to difficult depending on tools |

Project summary: Downed tree limbs as cache hides.

There are many different ways to accomplish the tree limb hide, and before we start it's helpful to consider some of the variables involved. If you can find a log that is hollow inside and not too rotted out, that would save a lot of time. If you have a half dozen power tools and a work bench out in the garage, then that too will make quick work of the woodworking part.

## General strategy

The general plan is to insert a waterproof container inside of a tree limb so that its visibility is obscured and the log plays a camouflage role for the cache, **Figure 12**. As mentioned, if you can find a small hollow log, then half your work is done already. All you would need to do is clear out and clean the core of the log and find a container that will fit.

If you have to start with a limb cut from a tree, the approach is to use a chain saw to cut a section out of the main branch, sawing it length-wise, and then hollow out a section to hold an internal container. You would attach that section back on with metal hinges, so it closes over the container. You can use a hand saw instead of a chain saw, but it will take much more time and effort.

## Specific plan

This particular project starts with a downed tree, and one limb is saved before it goes into the recycling bin. Don't try to tackle any limb more than 4 or 5 inches thick, unless you happen to have a lumberjack in the family.

Saw the stump lengthwise down the middle. Mark out a square on each half that is slightly larger than the container you plan to hide inside. You can mark with a felt pen, or if you have a rotary tool, such as a Dremmel saw, you can pre-cut an outline down to about ¼ inch. You need to leave at least ½ inch from each edge for structural purposes.

If you have a router you can make quick work of digging out a center hole. If you don't know what a router is, then continue with the chisel method.

Figure 12. A waterproof jar sits inside the wood cutout. The hinged door is held in place by a magnet and washer.

Use a new or sharpened ½-inch chisel. If you have not worked with a wood chisel before, then go slowly and read up on woodworking safety. You never want that chisel to be pointing towards you or one of your fingers. The other trick is to take out only small chunks with each pass.

Use a hammer to start at one corner of the outline. Bang it in about 1/8-inch all around the outline. Next place the chisel at one end and about 30-degrees and start to core out the center. Go slowly and carefully. A sharp chisel will cut out about 1/8-inch at a time with each pass. Time yourself as you go down into the wood in 1/8-inch steps. It's right about now that you may decide on using a much smaller container for your cache! The goal is to cut out a cylindrical bowl shape into each side.

If you're a neat freak, you can also buy a rounded, U-shaped chisel to make a nice smooth finish to the cut-out. You may also want to sand away the burs and splinters.

You will need to cut out both halves of the log. Once the cutout is big enough to hold your container, attach the two halves back again with metal hinges. Be sure to the edges line up nicely, so that when the flap is closed it looks like a solid log. You may need to spray paint the exposed cut edges to darken them to the bark color.

For my project I drilled a half-inch hole on one side and glued in a rare rare-earth magnet of the same size. On the facing surface I screwed in a metal washer as a contact plate for the magnet. This keeps the door closed, protecting the hide.

If you're like me, the two halves will not quite line up properly. Don't worry. This will be hidden in the woods with other branches and debris, and a man going by on horseback will never notice the minor flaws. If it's really bad, reinstall the hinges or use a lot of black spray paint to cover up the flaws. The whole idea is to make it fun for other geocachers, not necessarily to showcase your carpentry skills.

# 12. Birdhouse Conversion

A birdhouse makes a great hiding spot, as the container is already available, and most passers-by will think it's simply a birdhouse. Modifications are needed so one side opens like a door and a more waterproof container can be stored there.

| Name | **Birdhouse Conversion** |
|------|--------------------------|
| Description | Convert a birdhouse by adding a door |
| Pros | Good camouflage; quick and easy |
| Cons | Expense or labor |
| Appeal | Cute idea that everyone enjoys |
| Cost | About $25 new or $10 used |
| Time | Under 1 hour |
| Difficulty | Easy; use small hand tools |

Project summary: Birdhouse hides.

Birdhouses are like key chains: they are everywhere and a dime a dozen. Be sure to check your local discount centers. You can build a simple birdhouse yourself, but it can be difficult and time consuming, so I favor buying a well worn one in a thrift store. Try to find one where one wall will come out easily so you can make a hinged door to hide a cache inside.

In the example shown here there is no easy way to take out one wall without the whole structure collapsing, so an easy solution is to use a box saw to cut away one section of the back. Then you can pry the panel off and make a hinged door out of it, **Figure 13**.

Figure 13. A back panel is sawed open and pried off.

Use a punch to start the screw holes so it lines up properly. You may want to add some spray paint for protection to the exposed raw wood.

I also added a magnet inside mounted on a simple elbow bracket, **Figure 14**. The magnet attracts a washer glued onto the door flap to keep it closed. There is still plenty of room to fit a 6-ounce plastic container inside. I like this arrangement because you have an outer disguise, an inner waterproof container, and if you're a worry-wort you can also enclose the log in a plastic bag. That provides three levels of protection.

Be sure to add a piece of screening to the bird entrance or some kind of barrier to keep them out.

Figure 14. Use a punch to mark the hinge screw locations so that the door flap aligns properly. You can add a magnet inside and a metal washer so it stays shut in the wind. There is still room for the inner jar.

# 13. False Surveillance Camera

Surveillance cameras are everywhere. This project uses a false security camera as a cache. The fact that it is a camera will make most muggles shy away, but the quick-witted geocacher soon catches on to the idea that maybe it's just a clever hiding place.

| Name | **False Surveillance Camera** |
|---|---|
| Description | Hollowed out toy or used video camera |
| Pros | Looks like a surveillance device |
| Cons | May be hard to hollow out the insides |
| Appeal | Tricky and clever |
| Cost | $5 to $15 |
| Time | Under an hour once you find the camera |
| Difficulty | Easy |

Project summary: Empty security camera.

For this project I found a toy security camera that looks pretty real and opened it up to take out the insides, **Figure 15** top and middle. The top is a simple slide-off panel. I installed a hinge on one side of the top cover so folks can just flip up the lid to get to the cache contents.

The only hard part of this project is lining up the lid with the main body of the camera housing so that when you drill the holes for the hinges the top flips back down snugly.

Many security cameras, both the toy and genuine versions, are sealed by Phillips head screws, so these may have to be removed to provide quick access for the geocacher. Actually it's better to snip off the heads and replace them into the same holes and secure with glue, so it looks real from the outside. Again, the only skill required (and frustration factor) is getting the cover to line up properly when you attach a hinge on the side. The only advice I can offer is to drill the holes a little larger than necessary and use lock washers, so there is some wiggle room in attaching the hinge. Then you can fine tune the fit my loosening the bolts a little and jiggling the position.

If you can find a genuine security camera – you might find a broken one for just a few dollars – then that works even better, as it looks convincingly real (**Figure 15,** bottom).

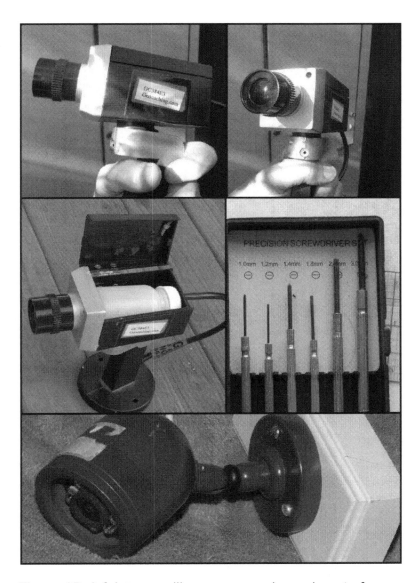

Figure 15. A false surveillance camera is made out of a toy, top. Precision screw drivers help take it apart. A real camera is hollowed out to make a hide, bottom.

Simply unscrew the cover plate. You'll see very small screws holding the guts in place. Undo those screws and remove the innards. For such jobs it pays to have a set of what are called precision screwdrivers. These are tiny Phillips and flat-head screwdrivers that computer techs use. The entire set is usually under $5.00. You may have to cut out a piece of black paper and place it onto the inside of the glass to hide the contents.

## Mounting

There are several ways to install the camera in its final resting place. I like to add magnets to the base to make it a quick pull-off mag-mount. I use magnets from the Internet and epoxy them into place in the base. You might also consider mounting it on a block of wood and then simply drill a hole in the top so it can hang with a simple nail. See the bottom photo.

# 14. Library Book

This is a really fun project. Most people will not expect to find a cache inside a book. There are several different ways to accomplish this. You can take a blank journal and transform the first few pages, and let the rest serve as the log book, with no hiding area. You can hollow out the inside of a thick book and make a hiding place inside, or you can simply buy a book where the hiding place is already made for you. The only down side is that you will have to find a librarian or shop owner to lend a hand with access and maintenance.

| Name | **Book Cache** |
|------|----------------|
| Description | Cache is in a library book |
| Pros | Very unique and clever |
| Cons | Need permission from library staff |
| Appeal | An opportunity to teach about geocaching |
| Cost | Between $10 and $20 |
| Time | About 2 hours plus library negotiations |
| Difficulty | Simple |

Project summary: Using a library book as a cache.

This cache idea was inspired by geocacher "40" and his GC16FNQ hide. This is a library book in the geocaching section displayed and labeled as a reference book. Once you open it up, there are several pages describing geocaching, its history and references, **Figure 16**.

The remainder of the pages make up the log book. This gem has earned several dozen favorite votes on the Geocaching.com page and serves as an educational tool at the local library.

Before you undertake this type of cache you will need to contact the chief librarian for the facility where you plan to place the book. Most institutions are quite happy to cooperate. They will add a reference number and label to the outside of the book and help you to find the exact space on the shelves where the cache will reside.

## Convert a journal to a cache

Most bookstores sell blank books and journals. These are easily converted into book caches. Simply plan what you want to display on the first few pages. The GC16NFQ sample cited above includes a brief history of geocaching and reference material. There is an explanation inside for those visitors who accidentally stumble upon the cache. If you want some simple descriptive material about the hobby of geocachng, refer to the Geocaching.com website for boiler plate text that you can use. It doesn't matter if the journal pages are lined or blank, but I have seen quite a few stamps, designs, drawings, and John Hancock type signatures, so I prefer the blank pages as opposed to lined.

Figure 16. Upper left: blank books and journals can be found at most bookstores and convert easily into caches. Images are of library cache GC16NFQ by 40.

A simple method is to print your customized material and paste it onto the first few pages. You will find the book does not close properly if you paste extra pages in, so consider cutting out one page, next to the pasted page for each page that you add. Add a label to indicate the start of the log pages.

Once the book is placed you will need to monitor it regularly as this type of placement subjects it to a broad audience, and many people don't know anything about geocaching.

## Buy an off-the-shelf book container

Several manufacturers make hiding places for keys and valuables, a kind of poor-mans safe. These hiding objects include what looks like a can of soda, shaving cream, or a book. The book hide includes a rectangular box hidden inside the book. Sometimes these are called book safes. This is pretty close to a ready-to-go cache. Many do not have spare pages for the log. You may have to add a small pad to serve as a log.

To find vendors for such books enter keywords "hollow books" or "book safes" into any search engine.

## Make your own hollow book

It's not too hard to make your own hollow book out of an old throw-away volume, **Figure 17**. The problem with using old books is that you have no pages for a log. If you want to try for a work-around for the log, such as adding a small roll-up log, that might work.

Figure 17. You can hollow out the inside pages of a thick book and glue the pages together.

Making a hollow book is relatively easy, if a bit messy. You will need lots of plastic sheeting or Saran Wrap, white glue, a brush, a craft knife or box cutter, and a metal ruler. It helps to have a thin cutting board too, and even a poster board cut-out that you can use as a template to mark out the borders of the cut.

Start by wrapping the front cover and the first 10 or so pages with the plastic and hold it in place with tape. Do the same for the last 10 pages. This is to protect the end pages; you don't want glue on them. Next, mix the white glue with water; about 3 ounces of glue and 2 ounces of water. You can use Mod-Podge in place of the glue mix. Use the brush to coat the three edges of the book that are not protected by plastic. Apply the glue mix liberally. Use a plastic sheet between the glued pages and the protected ends and place a weight on the book, such as 5-pounds of flower, until it's dry.

Once the central pages are dry, make a cut-out from a piece of cardboard that you can use as a template. This is for marking the cut out area. The cut should be at least 3 quarters of an inch from each edge. Don't try to cut more than 10 pages out at once. Mark the pages for the cut area and place the cutting board under 10 pages and cut out the hollow with the craft knife. Repeat until you are down to the protected pages at the back. Once you're finished, apply the glue mix to the inside of the box cut out, and again add a weight to the book until it is dry.

Add your custom intro pages and the log book and you're ready to go. As above, you will need the cooperation of a participating librarian or shop owner.

# 15. False Utility Box

Utility boxes, control panels, and wiring enclosures are visible everywhere in urban environments. They might be electrical junction boxes, water sprinkler controls, or telephone wiring panels. They all broadcast the same unspoken message: "Don't Touch!" And that's exactly why they make good hiding places for caches. A passer-by would never guess it's a geocaching container.

| Name | **False Utility Box** |
|------|------------------------|
| Description | Phony electrical utility box |
| Pros | Blends in well in urban environments |
| Cons | Often not waterproof; need 2$^{nd}$ container |
| Appeal | Fun disguise |
| Cost | Under $10 |
| Time | Under 2 hours |
| Difficulty | Moderately difficult due to hinge |

Project summary: A utility box that opens like a hinged door.

Real utility boxes often have electric wires inside and therefore they are sealed with screws or locks to keep the public out. In order to make the box look real, yet allow geocachers to open it without a screwdriver, we will need to add a hinge so that the front (or rear) panel opens easily. Then we will need to add a magnetic latch to hold it in place. **Figure 18** shows a utility box spray painted a dark color and mounted to a fence post. You'll notice the edges of the box have built-in connecting flanges, so you can screw it right onto any wooden surface. The screw on the front panel give the suggestion that the box is sealed shut, but it actually flips up and you can put a waterproof container inside. In the upper right section of this photo you can see the bathroom cabinet style magnet that keeps the door closed as it lines up with the two glued-on metal washers in the flipped up cover plate.

Adding the hinge and magnet can be cumbersome for someone not used to working with shop tools. The utility box itself can be made of metal or plastic. The plastic ones are easier to drill for adding the hinge, but they can crack too. The metal ones are sturdier, but harder to drill.

Both plastic and metal utility boxes are not very waterproof. They have coin-shaped punch-out holes designed to make it easy for the electrician to add pipes that contain the wires for the box. These pipes are connected to the box with standard slip-ring tubular hardware (lower photo, right) that connects the pipe to the utility box. That lower photo shows other types of utility boxes, both a plastic and a metal version.

These utility boxes are made to connect to metal conduit tubing, but simple PVC pipe is much cheaper and easier to work with. I often connect the PVC pipe to an elbow that makes it appear as if it's going into the wall or the wooden support, but it's actually just glued in place.

**Materials List**

- 1 wooden board or fence plank to mount the box.
- 1 electric utility box.
- ½-inch PVC pipe, about 6 inches long.
- 1 PVC ½-inch elbow.
- One slip-ring cylinder to connect the PVC pipe to the punch-out hole.
- 1 cabinet magnet holder, or refrigerator magnets that you can glue in place.
- Guerilla glue.
- 1 cabinet door hinge with connecting hardware.
- Electric drill for hinge mounting.
- Optional: Spray paint for camouflage; cabinet knob to help open the faceplate door.

**Practical matters**

Start by paying a visit to the electricians section of the hardware store, and take a look at the various shapes and sizes of the utility boxes you can use. Measure the inside space so you can choose a jar or container that will fit inside and provide better waterproofing.

You'll need to decide where and how the box will be positioned. If there is no wooden surface you can attach it to, you may have to pound a section of PVC piping into the ground like a tent stake and simply mount the box on that.

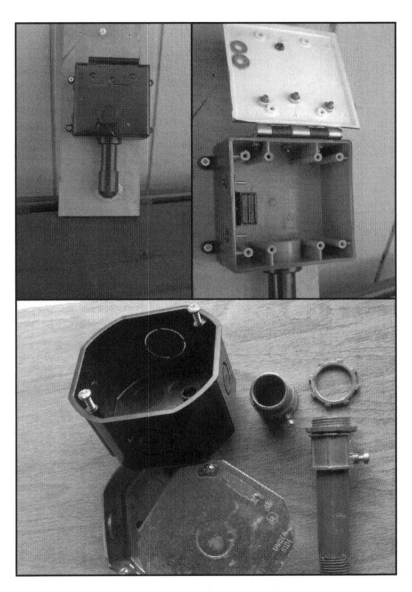

Figure 18. Utility electrical boxes blend in well.

The boxes have several "punch-out" holes. You will need to punch out one of these where the external pipe will be connected.

Look at cabinet hinges while you are at the hardware store. You will have to pick the size of the hinge to match a clear mounting side on the utility box. The cover plate to the box has screw connectors on the inside. You will need to snip off the screws and glue the heads into place. Then on the inside you'll see the sockets for the screws. These should be snipped about 1/8th inch too, and with any luck you can mount a small magnet there to hold the cover plate closed.

# 16. Magnetically Sealed Enclosure

The basic concept here is to use magnets to hold together the parts of an object that normally don't come apart. A 4x4-inch fence post, for example, is always perceived as a solid structure. This project uses two pieces of U-shaped wood pieces that are connected by magnets and when placed together they look just like a solid piece of wood. Of course you can use the same idea for metal panels, control boxes, or even a false branch on a tree.

| Name | **Magnetically Sealed Enclosures** |
|---|---|
| Description | Embedded magnets hold an object shut |
| Pros | Excellent form of concealment |
| Cons | The seam is often a dead give-away |
| Appeal | A popular hiding technique |
| Cost | Minimal: $10 to $20 |
| Time | About an hour |
| Difficulty | Moderate: Use hand tools and glue |

Project summary: Magnetic enclosures hold parts together.

The hardest part of this project is gathering all the supplies. You can probably find everything you need at the hardware store, but I often like to buy some items on line, so I can get a bulk discount. The wood I selected is a grooved timber used in fencing; these are readily available in most lumber yards. If you can find a variation on this type of pre-formatted wood, you might be able to find something with a larger interior cavity, so that you can hide a something larger than the bison tube shown here.

The magnets are best bought on line, if you have the patience to wait for delivery. Even a huge hardware store won't always have the fantastic variety of magnets you can find on the Internet. The Internet, meanwhile, has every conceivable size and shape, and you can buy several at a time.

There are four different types of magnets, but the most popular are the black ferrite magnets that you find in refrigerator magnets, and the more powerful Neodymium Iron Boron (NIB) magnets, commonly referred to as rare earth magnets. Both come in standard sizes, such as half-inch and 3/4-inch disks. **Figure 19**, top, shows three different disk magnets: a solid half-inch NIB disk, a half-inch NIB with a countersunk screw hole (on top of the drill bit), and a ¾-inch black ferrite disk on top of the ¾-inch drill bit.

A small 1/8th inch thick black ferrite magnet will cost between 10-cents and 15-cents when bought in bulk. A half-inch wide, 1/8th-inch thick NIB magnet will cost between 50-cents and 60-cents in bulk. Those with a hole drilled in the middle are near a dollar each, but the hole allows you to simply screw the magnet in place and avoid messy glues. Be careful with the NIB magnets: they are powerful enough to pinch a finger.

The easiest way to create a wooden enclosure with magnets is to drill a hole in the wood and use a mallet to pound the same sized magnet into the hole. For the opposite side on the facing plate, you can place either another magnet to match the first, or a simple metal disk that is attracted to the magnet.

Matching the two halves of the wood to each other is MUCH more difficult than it seems. This is due to three confounding influences.

1.  The magnets in each half (or the magnet and the attracting plate) have to match up exactly, or else the two halves don't sit right and this exaggerates the seam. Be sure to measure the center point on both halves exactly, then use a tiny drill (1/16th-inch) for a starter hole for the larger wood bit.

2.  You have to drill the wood hole pretty close to the actual thickness of the magnet. If it sinks in too far it may not attract the opposite side. If it's too shallow, the magnet will not be flush with the wood surface. Practice with the drill on a spare piece of wood in order to get the correct depth. If you drill down too far, partially fill in the hole with some glue and sawdust to raise the level.

3.  Even with a tight fit the magnet can come out of the hole, so you need to glue it in place. Glues and wood putty work OK, but they are quite messy. Consider buying the more expensive magnets with the countersunk screw hole in the center.

Figure 19. Magnets seal the container. Drill bits match the magnet sizes.

The photos I've enclosed show an early version of this project, with all the messy adhesives, misplaced holes, and sloppy craftsmanship, **Figure 19**, center. Despite all the errors it can still work decently, but you should at least *try* to make it look professional.

In mounting the enclosure in the field you may want to add a piece to the top to cover the hole, **Figure 19**, bottom, or attach a mounting stake to the enclosure so you can simply nail it in place onto a fence post.

Obviously, you can use the same magnet technique to clamp two parts of anything together in order to make a well camouflaged container. Magnets work well with plastic and metal containers although mounting the magnets on wood and metal takes more skill.

# 17. Concrete Mold

Concrete looks like stone, or may be made to look like rocks in a natural habitat, and that makes good camouflage for a cache hide. Concrete can be easily molded to any shape so you can hide a container inside. You can also piece together large chunks of discarded concrete to make a clever hiding place.

| Name | **Concrete Mold** |
|------|-------------------|
| Description | Make a cast around a container |
| Pros | Excellent camouflage |
| Cons | Heavy and labor intensive |
| Appeal | Not the prettiest, but good for a hide |
| Cost | Approximately $15.00 |
| Time | About 4 hours total |
| Difficulty | Difficult due to mess and failure rate |

Project summary: Use a concrete mold to hide a container.

## Concrete mold

You can take any container, cover it with wire mesh, and slather the whole thing with ready-mix concrete, and you end up with a blob that might look something like a rock or discarded building material, depending on your skill level.

WARNING: This is NOT the easiest way to camouflage a hide. The concrete is messy, heavy, and often takes a few coats to patch up the bare spots. Even then, sometimes large chunks can fall off or crack. You can achieve pretty much the same end product by simply buying a custom flower pot made of ceramic or clay, flip it over, and perhaps glue some stones on top, and it will be much less time consuming. Some of these flower pots are designed to look like rocks or natural formations, so they lend themselves well to geocaching hides.

Still, there are times when you may need a custom shape or a specific size, and making your own cover out of concrete remains a decent alternative.

Figure 20. A clay flower pot is covered with wire mesh then encased in concrete.

## Materials

You will need rubber gloves and a mixing container for the concrete. The trick here is that concrete is like very heavy toothpaste; it slips and flows. You have to prepare the object by covering it with wire mesh so the mixture has something to cling to. At the same time it's best to secure the wire mesh to some anchors on the underlying object. If you're in the hardware store, the wire mesh is usually displayed right next to the concrete mix.

**Figure 20** shows a small flower pot with the mesh covering the outside. I put a simple bolt and washer through the bottom hole of the flower pot and used that to secure the wire frame, bending the far end of the mesh over the lip of the flower pot. The bracket on the outside, barely visible at the top of the first photo, was intended to provide a hook so the whole contraption could be lifted easily. In patching up holes in the first iteration of this project, the hook got covered up. This is typical of the learn-as-you-go approach for folks like us.

The end product looks like a monstrous blob, but it works well. When it's dry, you'll have a rough-looking concrete surface that looks somewhat like naturally occurring aggregate rock. You may need to touch it up with spray paint.

Figure 21. Variations. Start with a hollow cinder block, or use a slab of concrete as a door.

## Start small

For your first project I recommend you try covering a relatively small container and no more than a half gallon of concrete mix, or about 6 pounds. The most common error in mixing concrete is adding too much water. Follow the instructions that come with the concrete mix. Some mixtures come in a bag and even provide a mixing tool.

Besides a flower pot, pretty much any small container will work. A good alternative is one of the steel or plastic switch boxes that electricians use. They are cheap and have screw holes that are good for securing the mesh.

## Variations

A variation on this theme is to start with a hollow cinder block and cover up one end of the opening, **Figure 21**. Another variation is to use found pieces of concrete that you can use as a flip-up door to hide something connected to a larger structure, bottom of **Figure 21**.

The easiest way to accomplish this is to drill holes in the concrete and attach a hinge. You will need special drill bits made for concrete. I reinforced the screws with gorilla glue. You will need to attach the other side of the hinge to an object in the field if you go this route.

# 18. Sheet Metal Cache Wrap

A cache wrap is a cheap and easy way to camouflage a container by recycling sheet metal art or decorations and wrapping them around the cache. Most thrift shops have copper plate, brass, tin or other metals that can be molded around a cache with a rubber mallet.

| Name | Sheet Metal Cache Wrap |
|------|------------------------|
| Description | Wrap-around camouflage for caches |
| Pros | Easy to apply, recycled items |
| Cons | Only partially covers the cache |
| Appeal | Easy way to bring interest to a cache |
| Cost | Often recycled materials so it costs little |
| Time | Under 1 hour |
| Difficulty | Easy |

Project summary: Sheet metal used for cache wraps.

This may be hard to explain, but when you see it you'll know it. Walk into any thrift store and you'll see these discarded, semi-antique wall and garden decorations that have seen better days. It may be an artistic tin-sheet fish or a cheap metal garden frog, but one look at it and you can see that with a snip here and some banging there you could cover that otherwise drab mayonnaise jar that you call a cache.

Many of these pieces are thin sheet metal supported by heavier gauge wiring. You may have to anchor the artwork onto your container using hardware or lots of duct tape, but it works. The best bet is to show some examples, **Figure 22**.

Figure 22. Tin and sheet metal floral decorations are used as wraps around a cache.

Once you find copper, sheet metal, or heavy foil materials, you can match them up with standard containers and use a rubber mallet to pound them into shape around the container, **Figure 23**. The matching to the inner container does not have to be perfect, but it should provide enough cover to obscure the view of the container, and it should be attached somehow. Zip ties, tape, and clue all work fairly well.

The advantage of this technique is that it can be used to provide a cover or mask for otherwise hard to conceal objects.

Figure 23. Bronze, copper and sheet metal can be used as a mask.

# 19. Hand Crank Electric Light

This project works by turning a hand crank that generates enough electricity to light an LED bulb. The LED is located several feet away from the crank and indicates the real location of the cache.

This is definitely a difficult and time consuming project, but if you want something truly "out there" then this is for you. If you're really going to try this, read the entire chapter first, as you may have to do some field research before you start.

| Name | **Hand Crank Electric Light** |
|------|------------------------------|
| Description | Crank lights up a bulb pointing to cache |
| Pros | Very odd; makes light with no battery |
| Cons | Somewhat difficult and time consuming |
| Appeal | Truly unique |
| Cost | About $30. |
| Time | About 3 hours |
| Difficulty | Requires soldering, mechanical skills |

Project summary: Generate light with a hand crank.

The hand crank generates about 3 volts of electricity, and you can choose to alter the output device to make different variations on this idea. The hand crank comes from an emergency radio or emergency flashlight. These cost between $10 and $15 on the Internet. The idea is to expose the rechargeable Ni-Cad battery pack in the radio, splice a parallel connection to that power source, and run an extension cable to another part of the forest. The far end terminates with an LED. The geocacher presses a switch at the radio location and looks around while turning the crank to try to see the LED. The extension cord must be run underground in PVC piping to another location where just the tip of the LED is exposed.

Pressing the switch will cause the LED to flash and lead the searcher to the cache. See schematic in **Figure 24**.

What you'll need:

- Emergency hand-crank radio/flashlight
- Miniature push-button switch (SPST)
- 3-volt LED light
- 20-foot or more extension cord
- 12-foot half-inch PVC pipe with two 90-degree slip-on elbow connectors; two straight connectors
- PVC cement
- Shrink tubing to cover solder connections
- 100-ohm resistor (brown, black, brown, gold)
- Mounting board for the radio and end connections
- Tools: Solder and soldering iron; wire stripper, hemostat or heat sink, hand saw; precision screwdrivers; small shovel.

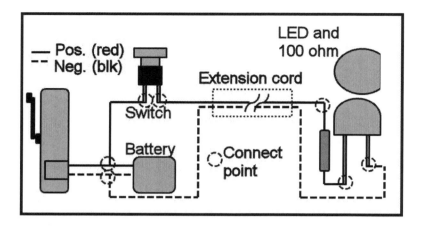

Figure 24. Wiring schematic. You can find LEDs with the limiting resistor pre-wired. Both the switch and the LED may come with mounting housing.

## Instructions: The Radio

Search around for an emergency radio or flashlight that features a hand-crank charger. I have seen these on sale for under $10 on the Internet, but it's best if you can find one in a store so that you can check whether the unit provides easy access to the built in Ni-Cad battery.

When you get the unit home, turn the crank and test that the radio/flashlight works OK. Check the flashlight assembly. If it comes apart easily, you may be able to gain access to the two wires that power the LED(s), and if so you can use this for the far end signal light. More often, though, you will have to use your own LED and tie it into the rechargeable battery.

Use the precision screwdrivers to open the latch covering the battery. You'll see the unit is connected with one red and one black wire. We'll need to splice into these wires and still be able to replace the battery into its storage area. This may require that you cut the wires and drill an access hole in the cover latch. In any case be sure to maintain the identity of the red (positive) and black (negative) leads, as the polarity of the LED is important. See the diagram and the photos below to help guide you.

Right now you have a red wire coming out of the radio and connected to the battery pack. You want to maintain that connection but add another wire that will eventually attach to one end the extension cord. It's best if you can find fine wires around your house, such as from a broken set of headphones or speaker wire. It would be best if you could find short pieces of both black and red wire. Let's assume you can find about 12 inches of red and black wire.

Cut the red wire about half way between the radio and the battery. Strip each end with the wire stripper to expose about ½ inch of copper. Do the same for the spare red wire, **Figure 25**. You can leave the battery cover latch ajar, or drill two holes in it to allow you to pass the red and black wires through it. Next twist all three red wires together and solder them together. Cover with shrink tubing or black electrical tape. Do the same thing for the black wires. Strip the other end of the red wire and solder it to one side of the push-button switch.

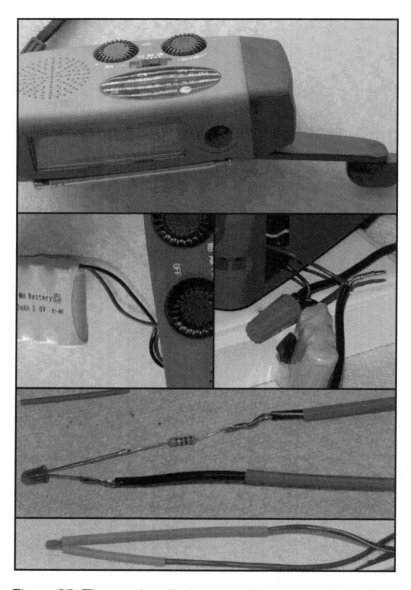

Figure 25. The crank radio is opened to access the Ni-Cad battery. Bottom: The far-end LED light must be wired with a resistor.

## Mechanics

It's not too early to start thinking of the mechanics of hiding the radio. You may want to consider mounting it on a small wooden plank or pole so that the hand crank is easily accessed yet sturdy enough to allow cranking without the whole thing falling apart. You can also use a bracket or a nail as a terminal point for the fine red and black wires where they will connect to the extension cord. Then you can use a plastic zip tie or electrical tape to anchor it all in one place.

Next, cut off the plug end and the socket end of the extension cord. Strip ½ inch of both wires at each end. If you're lucky you can find extension cords where one wire has a tiny white strip going along its entire length. You can use that to maintain the polarity of the red and black wires. Otherwise you have to carefully trace which side is which, so you know the positive from the negative end. Solder one wire to the other side of the push-button switch and the other wire to the black wire at the termination point.

## Instructions: The LED end

If the flashlight assembly comes off in one piece you can use that at the far end of the extension cord. Do not solder these connections just yet. Simply connect the wires from that to the other end of the extension cord by twisting the ends together being sure to observe the correct red-to-red polarity. We will need to test everything before making the connection permanent. More often than not, however, you will have to supply the LED and a 100-ohm limiting resister, **Figure 25**, bottom.

There are several options here regarding size and color. You can buy LEDs in holders for about $2.25 each and many come with the limiting resistor already wired in. For example, look for something like a 5-mm red LED, the Radio Shack Catalog #: 276-270. LEDs have polarity. The positive side is rounded and has a longer lead wire. The negative side has small flat facet and a shorter lead wire. To prevent the LED from burning out we have to add a 100-ohm resister to it.

At the far end of the extension cord, split the two wires and cut the negative (black) lead about 3 inches shorter than the other. Place shrink tubing on both ends; about 4 inches on the shorter end and about 3 inches on the longer end.

Place the hemostat on the short (negative) lead coming out of the LED. Solder that lead to one side of the 100-ohm resister. Next twist the exposed wire from the positive (red) side of the extension cord and attach that to the longer LED lead. Do not solder it just yet. Twist the negative wire from the extension cord to the unattached end of the 100-ohm resistor. Refer to the circuit diagram. Again, don't solder anything else at this end. You may have to use clips or tapes to keep the unsoldered connections in place.

## Instructions: Testing

We need to test that everything works properly. The flashlight and radio should remain off, and it might be wise to cover the dials in the off position with tape. Turn the crank for at least 30 seconds. Press the push-button switch. The LED should flash on and off with each push. If it all works OK go to the next section.

If the LED at the far end of the extension cord does not come on, recheck the twisted connections. If they look good, short out the two leads of the push-button switch with a piece of wire between the two leads and try it again. If it works then, the connections to the switch are bad. If it still doesn't work, disconnect the twisted wire connections at the LED end of the extension cord, and keep the bare wires away from each other. Next go back and check that the radio/flashlight works as when you first brought the unit home. If that doesn't work at all now, you may have messed up something in splicing into the Ni-Cad battery. Recheck all those connections, **Figure 26**.

If all else fails, use a DC volt meter. Place the black probe at the black wire solder connection by the battery pack and check each of the solders and connections along the red (positive) side. With several turns on the crank you should read about 3 volts at each station along the red wire until you reach the LED terminal.

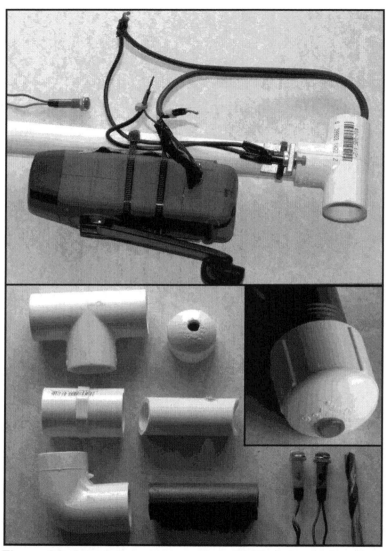

Figure 26. Attach the crank radio to PVC piping before the final soldering, top. Bottom image shows different PVC connectors and an LED embedded in an end cap.

## Field Installation

Once everything seems to be working, recheck your mounting options for the radio end. The wires from the extension cord will be emerging from one end of the PVC piping, so you may want to provide space to anchor the pipe and secure the wires to the connections going to the radio. Both the push-button switch and the LED can be purchased with mounting options. If you have room at either end for a plastic or metal plate, the components can be mounted into the plate by simply drilling a hole and tightening the hardware.

Next, scout out the field location you plan to use. Bring a tape measure and diagram the layout. If you can find two hollow tree stumps about 10 feet apart, that would be ideal. You will need at least one hollow or covered area to hide the radio end, and relatively soft ground for a trench to bury the PVC piping in. You may need to add length to the extension cord, which in turn requires more PVC piping.

Once you have the layout planned, come back home and cut the PVC piping into 3 or 4 pieces plus short sections for risers to come up from the ground, **Figure 27**. Disconnect the twisted wires from the LED end and thread the cord through the riser for the radio end, through the 90-degree elbow, and through each section of the horizontal run of PVC. Each place where the horizontal portion is cut you will need to add a straight extension slip-on piece to connect the ends. It's cut in sections because most people cannot fit a 12-foot pipe into their car. Be sure to sand ends smooth so they fit into the slip-ons easily. Continue threading the cord through the far-end elbow and up through the terminal end riser.

Now you can solder the LED onto that end of the cord. Before you solder the end wires, slip a 3-inch section of shrink tubing over the loose ends. This protects the exposed wire from corrosion and shorts. Use a hair dryer on the shrink tubing on both ends to make it contract over the solder joints. Black electrical tape works if you don't have shrink tubing.

Test the functionality one more time. Grab your supplies and tools and the PVC cement and head out to the field. Dig the trench between the hiding locations. Assemble and test it again in the field, and if it all works, apply the PVC cement to all the joints. Cover up the PVC pipe in the trench and add whatever camouflage you need to hide both ends. Give it a final test. Congratulations!

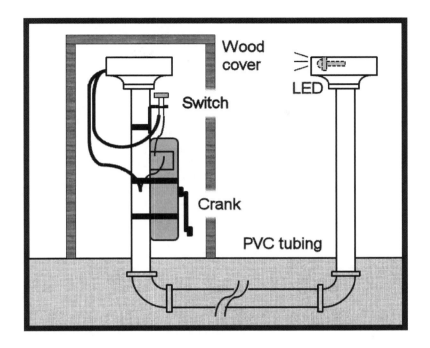

Figure 27. Mechanical layout of the crank and LED light has to be tested in the field.

# Appendices

## Geocaching Websites

THE major site for geocaching is Geocaching.com, the largest and most respected resource for this hobby. They also have an excellent discussion forum at forums.groundspeak.com/GC/.

Groundspeak is the umbrella organization for Geocaching.com, Waymarking.com (virtual caches), Wherigo.com, and CITO, the Cache-In, Trash Out adjunct to geocaching.

This and other website URLs are as follows

http://www.geocaching.com/

http://www.groundspeak.com/

http://www.waymarking.com/

Garmin:
http://www8.garmin.com/outdoor/geocaching/

Buxleys Geocaching Waypoint:
http://brillig.com/geocaching/

Open Caching: http://www.opencaching.com/en/

TerraCaching: http://www.terracaching.com/

Letterboxing: http://www.letterboxing.org

Handi-caching: http://www.handicaching.com/

## Magazines

FTF Geocacher: http://www.ftfgeocacher.com/

Online Geocacher: http://onlinegeocacher.com/

## Major Manufacturers

DeLorme: http://www.delorme.com/

Garmin: http://www.garmin.com/us/

Lowrance:
http://www.lowrance.com/Products/Outdoor/

Magellan: http://www.magellangps.com/

## Forums

Groundspeak:
http://gpsunderground.com/forum/forum.php

GPS Passion: http://www.gpspassion.com/forumsen/

GPS Review: http://forums.gpsreview.net/

## Participate

Do you have a great cache hide idea?

We're always looking for creative cache container ideas. If you have something you want to share, please feel free to send it in to us. If selected, we will include your project in the next edition of this book, and you will receive 3 free copies of the new edition.

Contact: FolsomNatural@aol.com. Send pictures, plans, and approximate costs.

49550139R00071

Made in the USA
Lexington, KY
09 February 2016